Instant 960 Grid System

Learn to create websites for mobile devices using the 960 Grid System!

Diego Tres

PUBLISHING

BIRMINGHAM - MUMBAI

Instant 960 Grid System

First published: September 2013

Production Reference: 1240913

Published by Packt Publishing Ltd.
Livery Place
35 Livery Street
Birmingham B3 2PB, UK.

ISBN 978-1-78328-073-5

www.packtpub.com

Credits

About the Author

Diego Tres has worked professionally since 2000, mostly with large global brands, such as Google, MasterCard, and PepsiCo. He has developed extensive technical skills in developing websites from designing to programming, and he is always aligned with a great business vision. He is always focused on frontend and is obstinate for perfection, seeking all the details involved in the execution of work to get the best results.

He was born in 1983. During his childhood, he joined a drawing course and also a painting course. After he broke his legs, he started playing keyboards in his samba group that he played keyboards. Later, he won a 586 computer from his stepfather, which included the famous software, Paint Brush; he then started gaining knowledge about Photoshop and HTML. In 1999, he published his first website using Microsoft Front Page and Macromedia Flash. His first job was as an instructor in web design; he began using web standards in the development of various applications and AJAX, and got a promotion in the same year. Later, he launched his first website for a global brand, Samsung. In 2007, he was selected as a finalist in the Grand Prix (London International Awards) for the first time. The very next year, he founded his own advertising agency; however, he unfortunately failed the first time due to the stock market crash. Later, he began using HTML5 and preprocessors, such as SASS and LESS. He also launched his website using responsive web design and Mobile First design. Recently, he had his name on a winning project. Now he enjoys animations with CSS, SVG, Canvas, and WebGL.

I would like to thank the team at Packt Publishing for inviting me to write this book. I would also thank my friends, my boss and friend Edson, my mom Rita, my stepfather Cloris, and my awesome brother Guilherme.

About the Reviewer

Afshin Mehrabani is a 21-year old web developer and an open source programmer. He is already a computer software engineering student. He started programming and web development with PHP when he was 12 years old. Later, he entered the Iran Technical and Vocational Training Organization. He received the gold medal in a country-wide competition on web development, and he also became a member of the Iran's National Elite'sFoundation by producing a variety of new programming ideas.

He was a software engineer at the Tehran Stock Exchange and now he is the head of the web development team in the Yara Company. He co-founded the Usablica team in early 2012 to develop and produce usable applications.

He is the programmer of IntroJs, WideArea, NPM.Vim, and some other open source projects. Also, he is contributing to Socket.IO, Engine.IO, and some other open source projects. His interests are in creating and contributing to open source applications, writing programming articles, and challenging with new programming technologies.

He has already written different articles about JavaScript, NodeJs, HTML5, and MongoDB, which are published on different academic websites. Afshin is already contributing to different startups, some of which will help to improve the open source community, making open source code easier and faster.

www.packtpub.com

Support files, eBooks, discount offers and more

You might want to visit `www.packtpub.com` for support files and downloads related to your book.

Did you know that Packt offers eBook versions of every book published, with PDF and ePub files available? You can upgrade to the eBook version at `www.packtpub.com` and as a print book customer, you are entitled to a discount on the eBook copy. Get in touch with us at `service@packtpub.com` for more details.

At `www.packtpub.com`, you can also read a collection of free technical articles, sign up for a range of free newsletters and receive exclusive discounts and offers on Packt books and eBooks.

packtlib.packtpub.com

Do you need instant solutions to your IT questions? PacktLib is Packt's online digital book library. Here, you can access, read and search across Packt's entire library of books.

Why Subscribe?

- ✦ Fully searchable across every book published by Packt
- ✦ Copy and paste, print and bookmark content
- ✦ On demand and accessible via web browser

Free Access for Packt account holders

If you have an account with Packt at www.packtpub.com, you can use this to access PacktLib today and view nine entirely free books. Simply use your login credentials for immediate access.

Table of Contents

Instant 960 Grid System

Welcome to *Instant 960 Grid System*. This book has been especially created to provide you with all the information that you need to create a responsive website using 960 Grid System. You will learn how to use grids, beginning with the layout in Photoshop to the final product in HTML; for example, building your own portfolio.

This document contains the following sections:

So, what is 960 Grid System? finds out what a grid is, how it can help you, when you can use it, and why designers and developers prefer to use only 12 or 16 columns.

Installation helps you learn how to prepare your environment to use 960 Grid System stylesheets from Photoshop to the files and folders of the project.

Quick start – using 960 Grid System from Photoshop to code lets you discover the real power of the 960 Grid System, positioning the elements of your layout in just a few minutes by just applying some classes in your HTML tags. Further, you'll learn how to apply the colors and sizes to your website in order to make it look as beautiful as a Photoshop version.

Top 3 features you need to know about 960 Grid System helps you learn the features of 960 Grid System In this day and age, where everybody owns a smartphone or tablet, it is unacceptable that we build a website which runs only on the desktop. Because of that, I'll teach you how to prepare your website for the present and the future with fluid grids, fluid media, and media queries, also known as responsive web design.

People and places you should get to know provides you with many useful links to the project page, as well as a number of helpful articles, tutorials, blogs, and the Twitter feeds of people to follow.

So, what is 960 Grid System?

On the Internet, Grid System was popularized by Nathan Smith, creator of the 960 Grid System, aka 960.gs—the most popular Grid System framework for building websites and rapid prototyping. You should use it every time you need to organize your content to build a website or when you need to build a rapid prototyping.

The modern grid, as we know today, was born after World War II, when some graphic designers began to devise a flexible system that would be able to help designers achieve coherency in organizing the page. Propagated mainly by Josef Muller-Brockmann in his book *Grid Systems in Graphic Design*, it is not hard to see the grids that have been used in the most popular websites on the Internet beyond print media.

One of the toughest decisions to make when you start with 960.gs is the number of columns you should use. The framework provides us with two variants: 12 or 16 columns.

The easiest way to decide which one to use is by asking the following question:

"Should my layout be divided by three?" If so, use 12 columns.

Don't worry if you didn't understand something. Sometimes, demonstrating is easier than explaining, and if you are like me, Grid System will be your best friend forever.

Installation

In four easy steps, you can prepare your environment to start with the 960 Grid System.

Step 1 – what do I need?

Before you start, you will need to check that you have all of the following required elements:

- **Code editor**: You can use any code editor you want as 960 Grid System supports HTML, CSS, and JavaScript. I preferred to use Sublime Text (`http://www.sublimetext.com/`) because it is light, flexible, and multiplatform. But feel free to pick the one you are comfortable with, for example, DreamWeaver, Coda, Textmate, Aptana, Visual Studio, Notepad++, Editplus, Emacs, Vim, and so on.

- **Graphic editor**: For this book, we used Adobe Photoshop. But 960 Grid System has templates for many graphic editors, such as Gimp, Illustrator, Corel Draw, Fireworks, and InDesign.

- **Browser**: I recommend Chrome because it is the fastest in my humble opinion and has great developer tools. But feel free to use what you prefer, that is, Firefox, Safari, Internet Explorer, and so on.

Step 2 – preparing the folders

Organization is everything. Before we start our project, we need to create our folders to receive our layout created in Photoshop, and we also need to create the HTML, stylesheets, images, and JavaScript that we'll need for our project.

Create the folders shown in the following screenshot on your desktop or any preferred path in your computer:

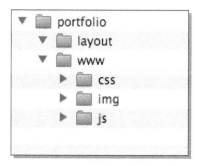

Step 3 – downloading 960.gs

The easiest way to download 960.gs is as a compressed package from `http://960.gs`.

On the site, click on **Big ol' DOWNLOAD button :)** as shown in the following screenshot:

Unpack the zip file and find the Photoshop template called `960_grid_12_col.psd` inside the folders `Templates/Photoshop`.

Copy this file to our folder `layouts` and rename it to `desktop.psd`. We will create the layout of our portfolio using this file as the base.

And inside the folder `code/css`, copy the files `960.css` and `reset.css` to our folder called `css`. These files will be used as the grid framework to our project.

Now, your project folder needs to be like the following screenshot:

Step 4 – linking the files

Now that we have all the 960.gs files we will use, it's time to link the files. To do that, we need to create our HTML file called `index.html` inside the folder www and link the stylesheets we downloaded before:

```html
<!doctype html>
<html>
  <head>
    <meta charset="utf-8">
    <meta name="viewport" content="width=device-width">
    <title>Portfolio</title>
    <link href="css/reset.css" rel="stylesheet" type="text/css">
    <link href="css/960.css" rel="stylesheet" type="text/css">
```

```
    </head>
    <body>
    </body>
  </html>
```

Downloading the example code

You can download the example code files for all Packt books you have purchased from your account at http://www.PacktPub.com. If you purchased this book elsewhere, you can visit http://www.PacktPub.com/support and register to have the files e-mailed directly to you.

And that's it!

By this point, you should have all the necessary files to start building your portfolio.

Quick start – using 960 Grid System from Photoshop to code

In this section, we will show you how to create your first website, similar to the following screenshot, based on 960.gs:

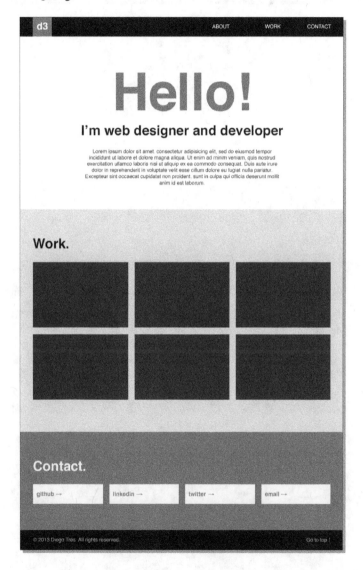

As you can see, my section **Work.** is divided into three sections (four columns per job), and because of that, I used the 12-column grid. If I have had used a grid with 16 columns, it would have been impossible to make this section, because it is not divisible by three. In this case, we should change our layout to use one or two or four or eight or 16 jobs per line.

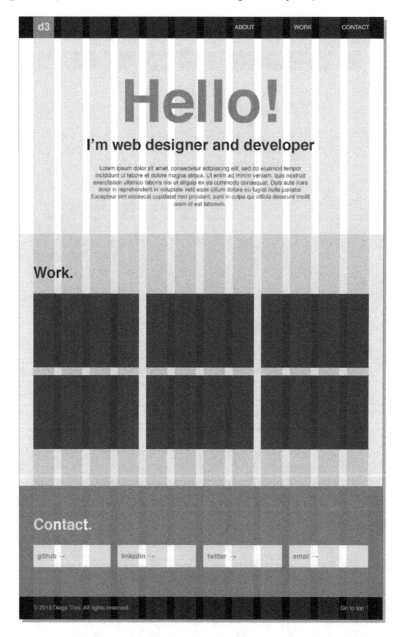

All the elements are totally aligned with almost no effort, as I will show you.

Step 1 – laying out in Photoshop with the 960 Grid System

Perform the following steps for laying out Photoshop with the 960 Grid System:

1. For the header, let's draw the logo with one column and the navigation items with six, leaving five blank columns between them.

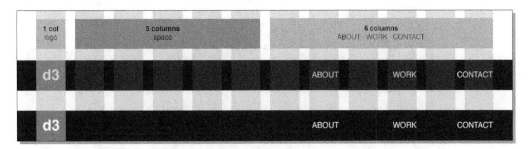

2. For the **ABOUT** section, let's use 12 columns for the title, 12 for the subtitle, and 8 columns for the text, with two columns for space on both the sides.

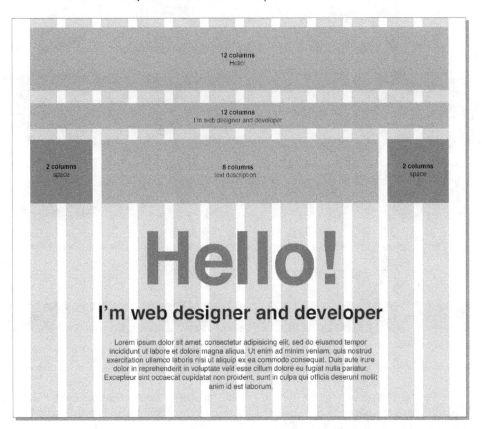

3. For the **WORK** section, let's use 12 columns for the title and three columns for each thumbnail. I think you will have picked this up quickly and won't need more red and green markers.

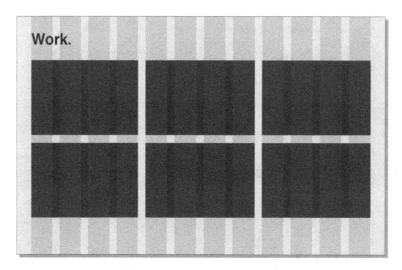

4. The **CONTACT** section is almost the same as the previous one:

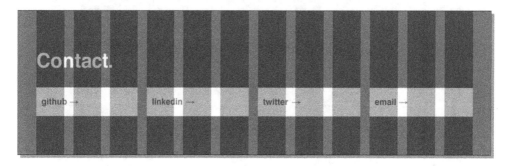

5. For the footer, let's use 10 columns for the copyright and two for the **Go to Top** link.

As you learned when you were using grids in Photoshop, it was not too necessary to think about in all the columns and spaces all the time. The most important thing here is learning how to read a grid file—always read in a line from left to right.

Step 2 – from layout to code

Now, we will learn the 960.gs stylesheet and how to convert the layout to code.

1. All the sections need to be a container class. In this case, `.container_12`. If we were using a layout with 16 columns, this class would have been `.container_16`.

2. After each container, we need add a `div` tag with the class `.clear` in order to clear the floats. If you need more information on this, please read the article at `http://sonspring.com/journal/clearing-floats`

3. Now we can work on the header section.

4. In this image, I've converted all the columns to 960.gs names.

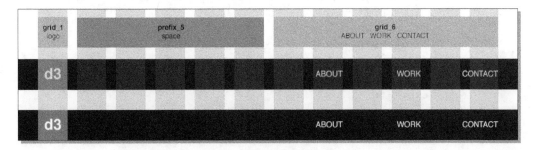

5. As you can see, `grid_1` represents one column, `grid_2` represents two columns, and so on. Let's see how it is represented in the code:

```
<div class="container_12">
  <h1 class="grid_1">
    <a class="logo" href="#">d3</a>
  </h1>
  <ul class="grid_6">
    <li><a href="#about">ABOUT</a></li>
    <li><a href="#work">WORK</a></li>
    <li><a href="#contact">CONTACT</a></li>
  </ul>
</div>
```

6. Add the space `prefix_5` to the element UL, which has five columns before it. In 960.gs, the name of this space BEFORE is prefix:

```
<div class="container_12">
  <h1 class="grid_1">
    <a class="logo" href="#">d3</a>
  </h1>
  <ul class="grid_6 prefix_5">
    <li><a href="#about">ABOUT</a></li>
    <li><a href="#work">WORK</a></li>
```

```
      <li><a href="#contact">CONTACT</a></li>
    </ul>
  </div>
```

7. And let's finish adding the tag header for the background, the links of the navigation, and the .clear class:

```
<header class="main_header">
  <div class="container_12">
    <h1 class="grid_1">
      <a class="logo" href="#">d3</a>
    </h1>
    <ul class="grid_6 prefix_5">
      <li><a href="#about">ABOUT</a></li>
      <li><a href="#work">WORK</a></li>
      <li><a href="#contact">CONTACT</a></li>
    </ul>
  </div>
  <div class="clear"></div>
</header>
```

8. Now, if you open the index.html file in your browser, it should look like this:

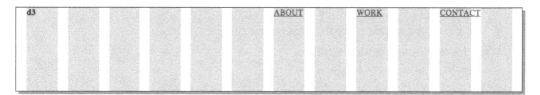

 Install the 960 Gridder System (http://peol.github.io/960gridder/) in your browser to see the grids in your HTML.

9. Let's do the same with the **ABOUT** section:

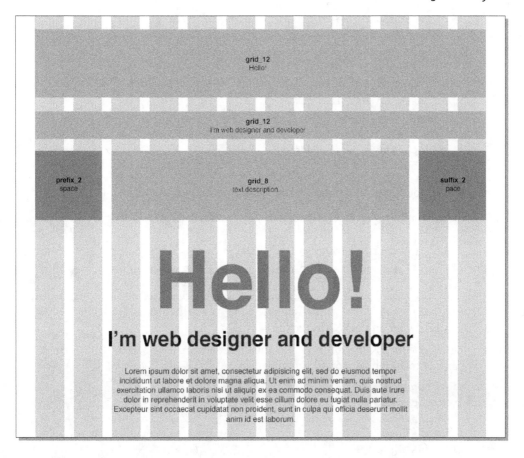

But now we have a space after `.grid_8`. It's not so hard. We need to remember that every container should always sum-up to 12. So, to fill the extra space after the element, use the class `.suffix_2`.

10. Let's see this in the code:

```html
<section id="about">
  <div class="container_12">
    <header>
      <h2 class="grid_12">Hello!</h2>
      <h3 class="grid_12">I'm web designer and
        developer</h3>
    </header>
    <p class="grid_8 prefix_2 suffix_2">
      Lorem ipsum dolor sit amet, consectetur adipisicing
      elit, sed do eiusmod tempor incididunt ut labore
      et dolore magna aliqua. Ut enim ad minim veniam,
      quis nostrud exercitation ullamco laboris nisi ut
```

```
        aliquip ex ea commodo consequat. Duis aute irure
        dolor in reprehenderit in voluptate velit esse
        cillum dolore eu fugiat nulla pariatur.
        Excepteur sint occaecat cupidatat non proident,
        sunt in culpa qui officia deserunt mollit
        anim id est laborum.
      </p>
    </div>
    <div class="clear"></div>
  </section>
```

11. Now, if you reload your page, you should see something like this:

12. Now let's work on the **WORK** section.

13. In the code for this section, nothing is new. Just add `grid_12` to the title `"work"` and `grid_4` to each holder of each image:

```
<section id="work">
  <div class="container_12">
    <header class="grid_12">
      <h3>Work.</h3>
    </header>
    <ul>
      <li class="grid_4">
        <a href="#">
          <img src="http://placehold.it/300x200">
        </a>
      </li>
      <li class="grid_4">
        <a href="#">
          <img src="http://placehold.it/300x200">
        </a>
      </li>
      <li class="grid_4">
        <a href="#">
          <img src="http://placehold.it/300x200">
        </a>
      </li>
      <li class="grid_4">
```

```
      <a href="#">
        <img src="http://placehold.it/300x200">
      </a>
    </li>
    <li class="grid_4">
      <a href="#">
        <img src="http://placehold.it/300x200">
      </a>
    </li>
    <li class="grid_4">
      <a href="#">
        <img src="http://placehold.it/300x200">
      </a>
    </li>
  </ul>
 </div>
 <div class="clear"></div>
</section>
```

 I'm using a service called `placehold.it` (`http://placehold.it/`) to avoid saving the thumbnails at this time. It's very useful when you want to prototype fast.

14. Reload your browser to see the new code applied:

15. We are almost there; let's code the **CONTACT** section now.

16. Again, there is nothing new in this section, we're just writing the code again for practice. Add `grid_12` to the title "`Contact`" and `grid_3` to each button:

```
<section id="contact">
  <div class="container_12">
    <header class="grid_12">
      <h3>Contact.</h3>
    </header>
    <ul>
      <li class="grid_3"><a href="#">github &rarr;</a></li>
      <li class="grid_3"><a href="#">linkedin
        &rarr;</a></li>
      <li class="grid_3"><a href="#">twitter
        &rarr;</a></li>
      <li class="grid_3"><a href="#">email &rarr;</a></li>
    </ul>
  </div>
  <div class="clear"></div>
</section>
```

17. If you don't remember the layout of this section, take a quick look:

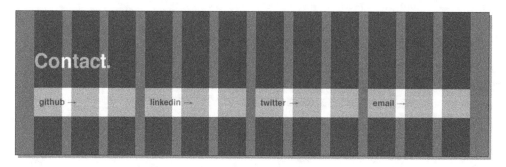

18. It's a piece of cake, isn't it? Let's update our browser again.

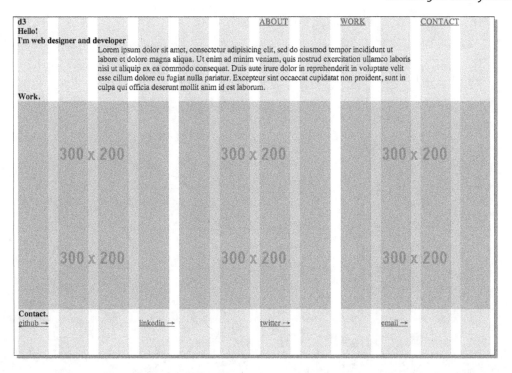

19. Lastly, let's code the footer section:

20. Add `grid_10` to the text on the left and `grid_2` to the text on the right. Remember always that the columns inside the `container_12` class need to sum up to 12.

```
<footer class="main_footer">
  <div class="container_12">
    <p class="grid_10">
      &copy; 2013 Diego Tres.
      <span>All rights reserved.</span>
    </p>
    <p class="grid_2 go_top">
      <a href="#">Go to top &uarr;</a>
    </p>
  </div>
  <div class="clear"></div>
</footer>
```

21. And tadaaaaaa! It's over. Let's update the browser.

While it certainly isn't the most beautiful website out there, nobody can say it is misaligned.

Step 3 – adding some colors, padding, and text alignment

As the basics of CSS aren't the focus of this book, let's start styling our elements together. First, we need to create another CSS stylesheet to store our styles.

1. Inside the `css` folder, create a file called `main.css`.

2. Before you write any line of code, link it to your `index.html` file beneath the place where you linked `960.css` before. Always insert the stylesheet files of the frameworks before yours, because it is better to overwrite the properties than to change the original file. This is how CSS works—in cascade.

```
<!doctype html>
<html>
  <head>
    <meta charset="utf-8">
    <meta name="viewport" content="width=device-width">
    <title>Portfolio</title>
```

```
      <link href="css/reset.css" rel="stylesheet"
        type="text/css">
      <link href="css/960.css" rel="stylesheet"
        type="text/css">
      <link href="css/main.css" rel="stylesheet"
        type="text/css">
    </head>
```

3.   Now let's identify the common elements.

4.   Identifying the common elements isn't the easiest task but I was able to do some. Inside your main file, `main.css`, write the common styles as shown in the following code:

```
/* common styles
=============================== */
body {
  font-family: helvetica, arial, sans-serif;
  color: #111;
}

a {
  text-decoration: none;
}

section {
  padding-top: 80px;
  padding-bottom: 80px;
}

h2 {
  font-size: 160px;
}

h3 {
  font-size: 42px;
  padding-bottom: 30px;
}
```

5. Now if you update the browser, your website will look a little better:

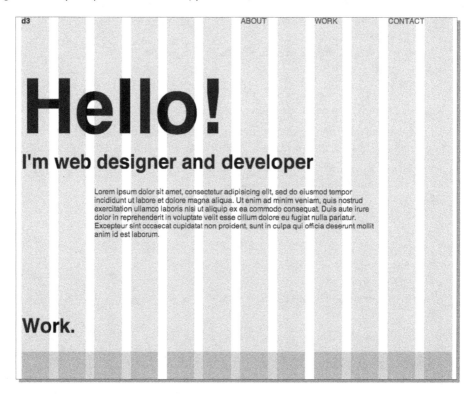

6. Now, let's work on the header.

7. In the same file, let's add the header styles:

```css
/* main header
================================ */
.main_header {
  height: 60px;
  background: #111;
}

.main_header .logo {
  float: left;
  width: 60px;
  font-size: 30px;
  line-height: 60px;
  text-align: center;
  background: #C00;
  color: #FFF;
```

```
    }

    .main_header ul {
      text-align: right;
    }

    .main_header ul li {
      display: inline;
      margin-left: 40px;
    }

    .main_header ul li a {
      line-height: 60px;
      color: #fff;
    }
```

8. Update the website again:

9. Now, let's see the **ABOUT** section.

10. In this section, let's just centralize the text and change the color of the title to red:

```
/* about
================================= */
#about {
  text-align: center;
}

#about h2 {
  color: #C00;
}
```

11. Reload your browser again:

12. And now, let's finish the **WORK, CONTACT,** and footer sections:

```
/* work
================================= */
#work {
  background: #ddd;
}
```

```
#work li {
  margin-bottom: 20px;
}

#work a {
  display: block;
}

#work img {
  width: 100%;
  height: auto;
}

/* contact
=============================== */
#contact {
  background: #c00;
}

#contact h3 {
  color: #fff;
}

#contact a {
  display: block;
  font-size: 18px;
  font-weight: bold;
  padding: 20px 10px;
  background: #fff;
  color: #c00;
}

/* footer
=============================== */
.main_footer {
  padding: 20px 0;
  background: #111;
  color: #999;
}

.main_footer .go_top {
  text-align: right;
}

.main_footer .go_top a {
  color: #999;
}
```

13. Now, we have a website that is aligned and beautiful.

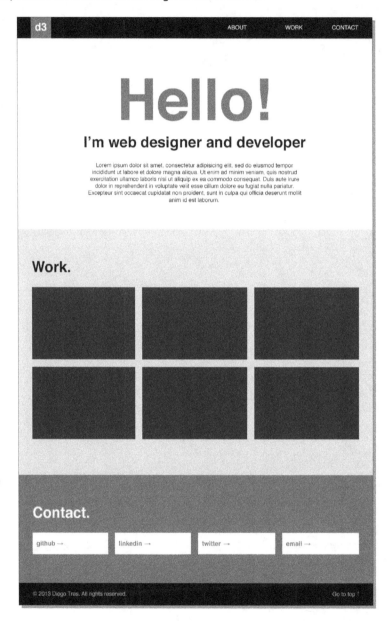

In the next section we'll learn how to make our portfolio responsive and capable of running outside the desktop.

Top 3 features you need to know about 960 Grid System

In this section, we will see how to prepare our desktop-only portfolio that runs in mobile phones and tablets.

Responsive web design

Nowadays, almost everyone has a smartphone or tablet in hand; this section prepares these individuals to adapt their portfolio to this new reality. Acknowledging that, today, there are tablets that are also phones and some laptops that are also tablets, we use an approach known as device agnostic, where instead of giving devices names, such as mobile, tablet, or desktop, we refer to them as small, medium, or large. With this approach, we can cover a vast array of gadgets from smartphones, tablets, laptops, and desktops, to the displays on refrigerators, cars, watches, and so on.

Photoshop

Within the pages of this book, you will find two Photoshop templates that I prepared for you. The first is `small.psd`, which you may use to prepare your layouts for smartphones, small tablets, and even, to a certain extent, displays on a refrigerator. The second is `medium.psd`, which can be used for tablets, net books, or even displays in cars.

I used these templates to lay out all the sizes of our website (portfolio) that we will work on in this book, as you can see in the following screenshot:

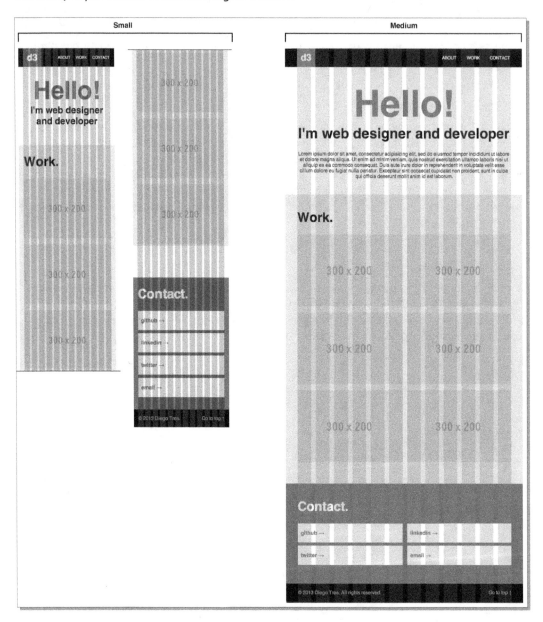

One of the principle elements of responsive web design is the flexible grid and what I did with Photoshop layout was to mimic those grids, which we will use later. With time, this will be easier and it won't be necessary to lay out every version of every page, but, for now, it is good to understand how things happen.

Code

Now that we have a preview of how the small version will look, it's time to code it.

The first thing we will need is the fluid version of the 960.gs, which you can download from `https://raw.github.com/bauhouse/fluid960gs/master/css/grid.css` and save as `960_fluid.css` in the `css` folder.

After that, let's create two more files in this folder, `small.css` and `medium.css`. We will use these files to maintain the organized versions of our portfolio.

Lastly, let's link the files to our HTML document as follows:

```html
<head>
    <meta charset="utf-8">
     <meta name="viewport" content="width=device-width">
    <title>Portfolio</title>
    <link href="css/reset.css" rel="stylesheet" type="text/css">
    <link href="css/960_fluid.css" rel="stylesheet"
       type="text/css">
    <link href="css/main.css" rel="stylesheet" type="text/css">
    <link href="css/medium.css" rel="stylesheet" type="text/css">
    <link href="css/small.css" rel="stylesheet" type="text/css">
</head>
```

If you reload your browser now, you should see that the portfolio is stretching all over the browser. This occurs because the grid is now fluid.

To fix the width to, at most, 960 pixels, we need to insert the following lines at the beginning of the `main.css` file:

```css
/* grid
================================= */
.container_12 {
  max-width: 960px;
  margin: 0 auto;
}
```

Once you reload the browser and resize the window, you will see that the display is overly stretched and broken. In order to fix this, keeping in mind the layout we did in Photoshop, let's start with the small version first.

The small version

In this version, we will cover the widths of containers up to 500 pixels; to do that, we will use media queries.

All the code we will type in this file (`small.css`) must be within the tag `@media`. So, let's write this important tag in the first line:

```
@media screen and (max-width:500px) {
   /* all the code must be here */
}
```

As you can see, it's not so hard.

Now, to make the design responsive and because, sometimes, we need to change the number of columns in each version, let's open `960_fluid.css` to let it guide us. We won't change this file; it's only for reference. To do this part, it is better to resize your browser to the width of a popular smartphone (something between 320px and 500px should be ok).

Header

Starting with the header, let's figure out what the differences are between the large and small versions in the following screenshot:

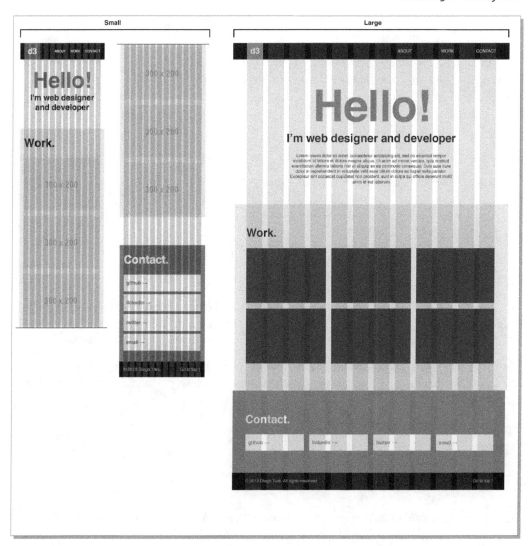

As you can see, our logo now needs more than one column. This happens because our columns are now narrower than in the larger version. Let's prepare the logo for three columns. To do this, we need to know the size of three columns in the fluid grid. Let's check them out in the `960_fluid.css` file.

If you scroll to 45th line, you will see the definition of the `grid_3` grid with the `container_12` container:

```
.container_12 .grid_3,
.container_16 .grid_4
{
  width: 23%;
}
```

Just copy this size of the width to our `mobile.css` file as shown in the following code:

```
@media screen and (max-width:500px) {
  /* main header
  ================================= */
  .main_header .grid_1 {
    width: 23%; /* match 3 columns in fluid grid */
  }
}
```

As you can see, we changed the width of the `grid_1` grid to that of the small version, but only for the `.main_header` scope. This means that for the `main_header` scope, from now on, one column has the width of three columns. This is how we will adapt to our layout.

Let's follow the same approach with the navigation menu, but, this time, in addition to changing the size of the columns, we need to remove the value of the class prefix and decrease the font size to `12px`:

```
.main_header .grid_6 {
  width: 73%; /* match 9 columns in fluid grid */
  padding-left: 0; /* remove prefix */
  font-size: 12px;
}
```

As you can see, a prefix class in the 960.gs framework is nothing more than `padding-left`.

About

In this section, we remove the large text and decrease the font size of the title and subtitle:

```
/* about
================================= */
#about h2 {
  font-size: 80px;
}

#about h3 {
  font-size: 30px;
}
```

```
#about .grid_8 {
  display: none;
}
```

Work

In this section, we want each image filling all the width. To do this, we need each image to have a width of 12 columns. Using the `960_fluid.css` file as the reference, we can see that 12 columns in the `container_12` container comprise 98 percent of the width of the containers in this version. Just copy the value to our context:

```
#work .grid_4 {
  width: 98%; /* match 12 columns in fluid grid */
}
```

Contact

In this section, we need to adapt our buttons to have the whole available width be the same as it is in the previous section. As we know, now that 12 columns represent 98 percent of width of the container, it isn't necessary to check the `960_fluid.css` file again. I added a little margin at the bottom to separate the buttons:

```
#contact .grid_3 {
  width: 98%; /* match 12 columns in fluid grid */
  margin-bottom: 10px;
}
```

Footer

To finalize the small version, we need to fix the footer:

```
.main_footer .grid_10 {
  width: 64.666%; /* match 8 columns in fluid grid */
}

.main_footer .grid_10 span {
  display: none; /* Remove legal text */
}

.main_footer .grid_2 {
  width: 31.333%; /* match 4 columns in fluid grid */
}
```

Now, if you reload and resize your browser, you will see a portfolio that adapts well to small and large screens; we just need to cover the space between them. But, now that you worked on the widths of the small version, the medium one will be a piece of cake.

The medium version

In this version, we will cover the widths from 501 pixels through to 800 pixels. So, as we did in the previous version, let's check the differences between the two versions, medium and large, in this case:

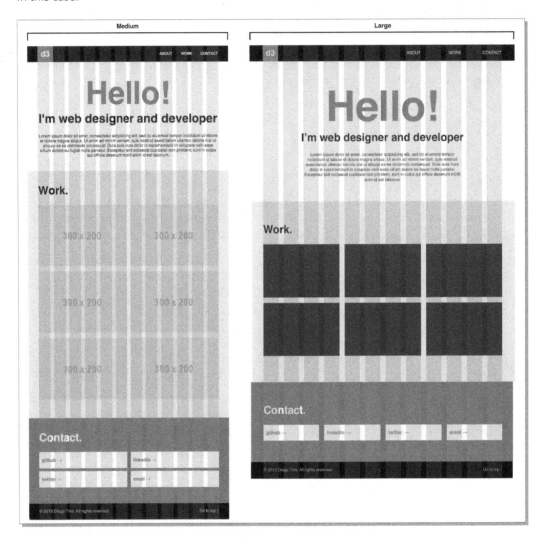

As you may have noticed, the size of the medium layout is pretty close to that of the large one. But, what we cannot see in this static layout of 768 pixels width is that, since this version need to cover the resolutions from 501 pixels to 800 pixels and we can draw only one of these almost 300 possible widths, it will have to adapt. As it is impractical to draw a version for each possible width in Photoshop, we have to draw the key resolutions wondering only about how the elements will behave in the other resolutions that we do not draw. *Trent Walton* from Paravel wrote a good article named *CONTENT CHOREOGRAPHY* which can be found at `http://trentwalton.com/2011/07/14/content-choreography/`.

Header

Starting with the header, I really recommend you use the same columns from the small version to support the widths at the beginning of this breakpoint:

@media screen and (min-width:501px) and (max-width:800px) {

```
    .main_header .grid_1 {
      width: 23%; /* match 3 columns in fluid grid */
    }

    .main_header .grid_6 {
      width: 73%; /* match 9 columns in fluid grid */
      padding-left: 0; /* remove prefix */
      font-size: 14px;
    }

    .main_header ul li {
      margin-left: 30px;
    }
  }
}
```

As you may have noticed in the first line, we're using a media query with a range of widths `501px` through to `800px`:

@media screen and (min-width:501px) and (max-width:800px)

Further, we set the font size of the menu to `14px` and the spaces between the menu items to `30px`.

About

In this section, let's improve the font sizes and set the width of the large text to 12 columns:

```
#about h2 {
  font-size: 120px;
}

#about h3 {
  font-size: 46px;
}

#about .grid_8 {
  width: 98%; /* match 12 columns in fluid grid */
  padding-left: 0; /* remove prefix */
  padding-right: 0; /* remove suffix */
}
```

Moreover, we removed the `prefix` and `suffix` classes, and, as you may have noticed, the `suffix` class is just a `padding-right`.

Work

As our layout is medium sized, let's set the columns in the `work` section to six in order to have two images per line:

```
#work .grid_4 {
  width: 48%; /* match 6 columns in fluid grid */
}
```

Now, set the columns for the `contact` section.

Contact

As we did in the previous section, we want two elements per line with a little margin at the bottom of the containers to separate them:

```
#contact .grid_3 {
  width: 48%; /* match 6 columns in fluid grid */
  margin-bottom: 10px;
}
```

Footer

Now we have enough space, so we won't hide the legal text. We just need to make a simple adjustment in the columns from grid_10 to grid_9 on the left side of the column and from grid_2 to grid_3 in the link on the right side of the column:

```
.main_footer .grid_10 {
   width: 73%;   /* match 9 columns in fluid grid */
}


.main_footer .grid_2 {
   width: 23%;   /* match 3 columns in fluid grid */
}
```

Reload your browser for the last time and that is it. You should have a portfolio running in all the screen sizes.

People and places you should get to know

If you need help with 960 Grid System, the following sections tell you about some people and places that will prove invaluable.

Official sites

+ Homepage of 960.gs: `http://960.gs/`

+ Download: `http://github.com/nathansmith/960-Grid-System/zipball/master`

+ Demo: `http://960.gs/demo.html`

+ Slides: `https://speakerdeck.com/nathansmith/960-grid-system`

+ Source code: `https://github.com/nathansmith/960-Grid-System`

Articles and tutorials

+ Web Designer Depot's featured article, *Fight Div-itis and Class-itis With the 960 Grid System*, on writing less code by styling the tags directly: `http://www.webdesignerdepot.com/2010/03/fight-div-itis-and-class-itis-with-the-960-grid-system/`

+ *Prototyping With The Grid 960 CSS Framework*—a great net tuts+ article: `http://net.tutsplus.com/tutorials/html-css-techniques/prototyping-with-the-grid-960-css-framework/`

+ The *Mastering the 960 Grid System* article by net tuts+: `http://net.tutsplus.com/tutorials/html-css-techniques/mastering-the-960-grid-system/`

+ The *The 960 Grid System Made Easy* article by *Joshua Johnson*: `http://sixrevisions.com/web_design/the-960-grid-system-made-easy/`

+ The *Tutorial for the 960 Grid System CSS Framework* article by *Professor Zac Gordon*: `http://dabrook.org/blog/tutorial-for-the-960-grid-system-css-framework`

Blogs

+ The blog by *Nathan Smith*, the creator of 960.gs: `http://sonspring.com/journal`

+ Smashing Magazine: `http://www.smashingmagazine.com/`

+ The blog by *Trent Walton*: `http://trentwalton.com/`

+ The blog by *Brad Frost*: `http://bradfrostweb.com/blog/`

+ The blog by *Luke Wroblewsky*: `http://www.lukew.com/ff/`

Twitter

- ✦ Follow *Nathan Smith*: `https://twitter.com/nathansmith`
- ✦ Follow *Luke Wroblewski*: `https://twitter.com/lukew`
- ✦ Follow *Trent Walton*: `https://twitter.com/trentwalton`
- ✦ For more open source information, follow Packt Publishing at `http://twitter.com/#!/packtopensource`

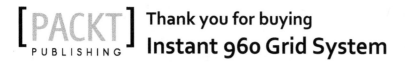

About Packt Publishing

Packt, pronounced 'packed', published its first book "*Mastering phpMyAdmin for Effective MySQL Management*" in April 2004 and subsequently continued to specialize in publishing highly focused books on specific technologies and solutions.

Our books and publications share the experiences of your fellow IT professionals in adapting and customizing today's systems, applications, and frameworks. Our solution based books give you the knowledge and power to customize the software and technologies you're using to get the job done. Packt books are more specific and less general than the IT books you have seen in the past. Our unique business model allows us to bring you more focused information, giving you more of what you need to know, and less of what you don't.

Packt is a modern, yet unique publishing company, which focuses on producing quality, cutting-edge books for communities of developers, administrators, and newbies alike. For more information, please visit our website: www.packtpub.com.

Writing for Packt

We welcome all inquiries from people who are interested in authoring. Book proposals should be sent to author@packtpub.com. If your book idea is still at an early stage and you would like to discuss it first before writing a formal book proposal, contact us; one of our commissioning editors will get in touch with you.

We're not just looking for published authors; if you have strong technical skills but no writing experience, our experienced editors can help you develop a writing career, or simply get some additional reward for your expertise.

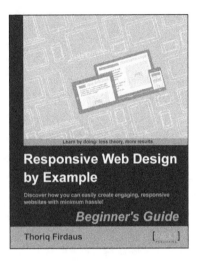

Responsive Web Design by Example

ISBN: 978-1-84969-542-8   Paperback: 338 pages

Discover how you can easily create engaging, responsive websites with minimum hassle!

1. Rapidly develop and prototype responsive websites by utilizing powerful open source frameworks

2. Focus less on the theory and more on results, with clear step-by-step instructions, previews, and examples to help you along the way

3. Learn how you can utilize three of the most powerful responsive frameworks available today: Bootstrap, Skeleton, and Zurb Foundation

Drupal 7 Mobile Web Development Beginner's Guide

ISBN: 978-1-84951-562-7   Paperback: 338 pages

Transform your existing Drupal site into one that is completely compatible with mobile and tablet devices

1. Follow the example of a 'Mom & Pop' restaurant site to make the transition to a mobile site easier

2. Prototype a distributed team workflow with GIT version control

3. Implement audio, video, charting and mapping solutions that work on Mobile, Tablet, and Desktop browsers

Please check **www.PacktPub.com** for information on our titles

PUBLISHING

Responsive Web Design
with HTML5 and CSS3

Learn responsive design using HTML5 and CSS3 to adapt
websites to any browser or screen size

Ben Frain

[PACKT]

Responsive Web Design with HTML5 and CSS3

ISBN: 978-1-84969-318-9   Paperback: 324 pages

Learn responsive design using HTML5 and CSS3 to adapt
websites to any browser or screen size

1. Everything needed to code websites in HTML5
    and CSS3 that are responsive to every device or
    screen size

2. Learn the main new features of HTML5 and
    use CSS3's stunning new capabilities including
    animations, transitions and transformations

3. Real world examples show how to progressively
    enhance a responsive design while providing fall
    backs for older browsers

INSTANT
Short | Fast | Focused

HTML5 Responsive
Table Design How-to

Present your data anywhere on any device using responsive
design techniques

Fernando Monteiro

[PACKT]

Instant HTML5 Responsive Table Design How-to

ISBN: 978-1-84969-726-2   Paperback: 58 pages

Present your data anywhere on any device using
responsive design techniques

1. Learn something new in an Instant! A short, fast,
    focused guide delivering immediate results.

2. Optimize and visualize your data using responsive
    design techniques

3. Understand how responsive design works and
    which elements you should use to make your tables
    responsive

Please check **www.PacktPub.com** for information on our titles